dabblelab

10-MINUTE
KITCHEN
SCIENCE
PROJECTS

BY ELSIE OLSON

CAPSTONE PRESS
a capstone imprint

Dabble Lab is published by Capstone Press, a Capstone imprint.
1710 Roe Crest Drive, North Mankato, Minnesota 56003
capstonepub.com

Library of Congress Cataloging-in-Publication Data
Names: Olson, Elsie, author. | Makuc, Lucy, illustrator.
Title: 10-minute kitchen science projects / by Elsie Olson ; [illustrated by] Lucy Makuc. Other titles: Ten minute kitchen science projects
Description: North Mankato, Minnesota : Dabble Lab/Capstone Press, a Capstone imprint, [2022] | Series: 10-minute makers | Includes bibliographical references. | Audience: Ages 8-11 | Audience: Grades 4-6 | Summary: "Looking for quick and easy science projects for your makerspace? Look no further! From mini rockets and rainbows to ice cream and invisible ink, these amazing 10-minute kitchen science projects will have kids making in no time!"– Provided by publisher.
Identifiers: LCCN 2021029950 (print) | LCCN 2021029951 (ebook) | ISBN 9781663959010 (hardcover) | ISBN 9781666322088 (pdf) | ISBN 9781666322101 (kindle edition)
Subjects: LCSH: Science–Experiments–Juvenile literature. | Science projects–Juvenile literature.
Classification: LCC Q164 .O47 2022 (print) | LCC Q164 (ebook) | DDC 507.8–dc23
LC record available at https://lccn.loc.gov/2021029950
LC ebook record available at https://lccn.loc.gov/2021029951

Image Credits
Project photos: Mighty Media, Inc.
iStockphoto, p. 16 (hand)

Design Elements
Shutterstock Images

Editorial Credits
Editor: Liz Salzmann
Production Specialist: Aruna Rangarajan

Printed and bound in the USA. PO4608

TABLE OF CONTENTS

GOT 10 MINUTES?

Turn your kitchen into a laboratory with these quick and easy science projects and experiments. Make a test-tube rainbow, a bottle rocket, and more. Have fun and get messy! These projects are so quick, you'll have plenty of time to clean up your lab when you're finished!

General Supplies and Tools

baking soda

cotton swabs

flour

food coloring

gummy candy

jelly beans

lemons

milk

salt

shaving cream

test tubes

vinegar

Tips

- Before starting a project, read the instructions. Then gather the supplies and tools you'll need.

- While the active portion of each project takes 10 minutes or less, some may need to sit for a day or two. Make sure to put experiments in progress in a safe place!

- Ask an adult to help you with sharp or hot tools.

- The measurements for some experiments may need to be adjusted depending on the exact ingredients you are using.

- Change things up! Don't be afraid to make these projects your own.

TIE-DYED MILK

When you add dish soap to milk, the molecules in the soap race to join up with fat molecules in the milk. Add food coloring to see this science in action!

What You Need:

pie pan

2% or whole milk

ruler

food coloring

dish soap

small dish

cotton swab

What You Do:

1 Pour milk into the pie pan until it is about ¾ inch (2 centimeters) deep.

2 Add drops of food coloring in different colors.

3 Put a little dish soap in a small dish. Dip the cotton swab into the soap. Then touch the swab to one of the color drops.

4 Watch the colors dart apart and mix back together!

TIP Try using primary colors. These are red, blue, and yellow. What colors are created when primary colors mix together?

PIRATE TREASURE

Coffee grounds, salt, and water dry into solid stones perfect for hiding treasure. Scatter some around the yard and see if your friends can find them!

What You Need:

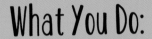

mixing bowl & spoon

salt

flour

coffee grounds

water

waxed paper

baking sheet

gems, beads, or other "treasure"

What You Do:

1. Mix together 1 cup (0.24 liters) of salt, 2½ cups (0.6 L) of flour, 2 cups (0.5 L) of coffee grounds, and 1 cup (0.24 L) of water. You should be able to mold the mixture with your hands. Add more water or flour as needed.

2. Spread a piece of waxed paper on a baking sheet.

3. Roll a clump of the mixture into a small ball. Press down in the middle of the ball to make an indent. Place the ball on the baking sheet and put a few gems or beads in the indent. Repeat to make more balls of treasure.

4. Cover the treasure in each ball with more of the mixture. Squeeze and mold each ball so it looks like a rock.

5. Allow the rocks to dry for a few days, then break them open to find your treasure!

TIP You can use used coffee grounds for this project. Start with a bit less water if the grounds are wet. Add more water as needed.

SQUASH BOWL

You can make papier-mâché glue with flour and water.
Use it and a squash to mold a clever kitchen bowl.

What You Need:

newspaper

ruler

scissors

squash

plastic wrap

measuring cups

flour

water

mixing bowl

spoon

paint & paintbrush (optional)

What You Do:

1 Cut or tear newspaper into strips about 1 to 2 inches (2.5 to 5 cm) wide and 4 inches (10 cm) long.

2 Cover the squash with plastic wrap.

3 Put 1 cup (0.24 L) of flour and 1½ cups (0.35 L) of water in a mixing bowl. Stir. Add more flour or water as needed until the mixture is about as thick as pancake batter.

4 Coat a strip of newspaper with the mixture. Use your fingers to remove excess mixture. Place the strip on the plastic-covered squash. Repeat until about half the squash is covered.

5 Allow your bowl to dry. Then carefully remove the squash and trim off the excess plastic wrap. Paint your bowl if you like!

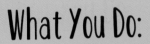

TEST TUBE RAINBOW

Adding sugar to water changes its density. More sugar makes the water denser. Try this colorful experiment to see layers of density!

What You Need:

4 plastic cups

tablespoon

sugar

warm water

food coloring
(not the gel kind)

spoon

test tubes

eye dropper

jar with lid
(optional)

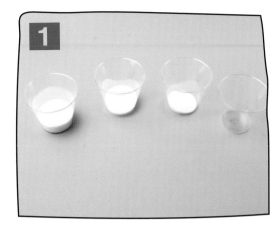

What You Do:

1 Set the cups in a row. Put 3 tablespoons (45 milliliters) of sugar in the first cup. Put 2 tablespoons (30 mL) in the second cup. Put 1 tablespoon (15 mL) in the third cup. Leave the fourth cup empty.

2 Pour an equal amount of warm water into each cup.

3 Add one drop of food coloring to each cup. Put a different color in each cup.

4 Stir the liquid in each cup until the sugar is dissolved.

5 Use an eye dropper to put water from each cup in the test tube. Add it in order from the water with the most sugar to the water with the least sugar.

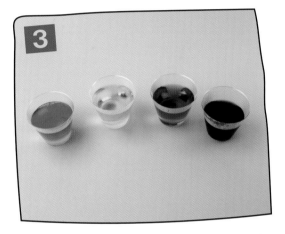

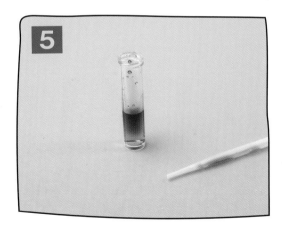

TIP To get the sugar to dissolve more quickly, put the sugar and water in a jar with a lid and shake it.

13

JELLY BEAN STRIPES

The dye used to color jelly beans can also color clothing!
Use candy color to jazz up an old shirt.

What You Need:

jelly beans

bowls

warm water

ruler

old T-shirt

baking dish

eye dropper

What You Do:

1 Sort the jelly beans by color. Put each color in its own bowl.

2 Pour warm water in each bowl until the jelly beans are covered by about 1 inch (2.5 cm). Wait two or three minutes until the water is colored.

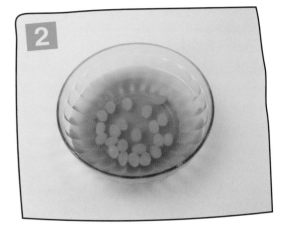

3 Lay your T-shirt in the baking dish.

4 Use the eye dropper to drip the colored water onto the shirt in stripes or other patterns!

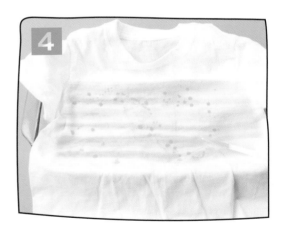

5 Let the shirt dry before wearing it.

TIP When you wash your shirt, the color may come out. That just means you can decorate the shirt again and again!

CHOPSTICK MAGIC

Step right up and amaze your friends by lifting
a heavy bottle of rice with nothing but a chopstick!

What You Need:

empty plastic bottle

uncooked rice

funnel

chopstick

What You Do:

1 Use the funnel to fill the bottle with rice.

2 Tap the bottle on your work surface a few times so the rice settles. Add more rice until the bottle is nearly full.

3 Push the chopstick into the rice until it hits the bottom of the bottle. You may need to wiggle the chopstick a little as you push it down.

4 Lift the chopstick to try to pick up the bottle. If the chopstick comes out, push it back in and wiggle it down toward the bottom. Try lifting the bottle again. Repeat until the chopstick lifts the bottle like magic!

TIP You may have to push the chopstick into the bottle many times. Don't give up! Each time you push the chopstick back in, it compresses the rice. Eventually, the rice will be solid enough to hold the chopstick in place.

GROWING GUMMIES

Osmosis is a process in which water molecules move from a substance with a greater concentration of water to one with a lower concentration. Watch osmosis in action with this fun gummy experiment!

What You Need:

3 small bowls

tape

marker

measuring cups

water

salt

sugar

spoon

gummies

notebook

pencil

What You Do:

1 Label the bowls "plain water," "salt water," and "sugar water."

2 Pour an equal amount of lukewarm water into each bowl. Add about ¼ cup (60 mL) of salt to the "salt" bowl and ¼ cup (60 mL) of sugar to the "sugar" bowl. Stir the liquid in each bowl until the salt and sugar dissolve. When you dip your finger in the water, it should feel gritty. Add more salt or sugar if needed.

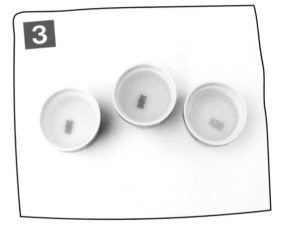

3 Place a gummy in each bowl. Let the gummies sit overnight.

4 Observe your gummies. How did they change? Write your results in a notebook.

TIP Using warm water will help the salt and sugar dissolve more easily. But if the water is too warm, it will melt the gummies!

19

FOOD DYE SLIME

Since ancient times, people have used natural elements to make dye. Some of these elements might be in your kitchen cupboard! Use them to make colorful slime.

What You Need:

- colorful berries or spices
- bowls
- measuring cups & spoons
- school glue
- baking soda
- water
- shaving cream
- spoons
- saline contact lens solution (make sure it contains boric acid)

What You Do:

1 If you're using berries, crush them in a small bowl.

2 Mix ⅔ cup (158 mL) of school glue, ½ teaspoon (2.5 mL) of baking soda, and ¼ cup (59 mL) of water in a large bowl.

3 Stir in 2½ cups (0.6 L) of shaving cream. Divide the mixture into smaller bowls to make multiple colors.

4 Stir in your colorful berries or spices until each mixture is the color you want.

TIP Turmeric works well to make yellow slime. Paprika is great for orange slime.

5 Stir in saline solution ½ teaspoon (2.5 mL) at a time until each mixture is a sticky ball.

6 Knead each mixture for several minutes until they turn into smooth, stretchy slime. It will be sticky at first! If it stays too thin or sticky, add more saline solution.

21

ICE CREAM IN A FLASH

Salt lowers the freezing point of water. By adding salt to a bag of ice, the ice gets colder, making it the perfect environment to create a sweet treat!

What You Need:

- measuring cups & spoons
- sugar
- milk
- heavy cream
- vanilla
- plastic zipper bags (quart and gallon sizes)
- food coloring
- ice
- salt
- spoon
- bowl
- towel or gloves (optional)

What You Do:

1 Put ¼ cup (59 mL) of sugar, ½ cup (118 mL) of milk, ½ cup (118 mL) of heavy cream, and 1 teaspoon (5 mL) of vanilla in a quart-sized bag. Add a few drops of food coloring in different colors. Tightly seal the bag.

2 Put 2 cups (0.47 L) of ice in a gallon-sized bag. Add ¾ cup (177 mL) of salt.

3 Place the quart bag in the gallon bag. Tightly seal the gallon bag.

4 Gently shake and rock the bags back and forth for about eight minutes, until the liquid in the quart bag has thickened into soft ice cream.

5 Put your ice cream in a bowl and taste your homemade treat! Notice how the different colors you added mixed together. Did you make a new color?

TIP The bag might get cold while you shake it. Wear gloves or use a towel to protect your hands if they get chilly!

SALTY STARS

Did you know that salt is a mineral? The type of salt we eat is in crystal form. Use the power of evaporation to create stars covered with sparkly salt crystals!

What You Need:

- card stock (multiple colors)
- pencil
- scissors
- shallow pan or dish
- measuring cups & spoons
- bowl
- salt
- warm water
- spoon
- string and tape (optional)

What You Do:

1 Draw or trace a star shape onto card stock. Cut it out. Use this star as template to make more card stock stars in different colors.

2 Arrange the stars in a shallow pan.

3 Mix together 4 tablespoons (59 mL) of salt and 1 cup (0.24 L) of warm water. Stir until the salt is dissolved. Pour the solution into the pan so the stars are just covered. Make more solution if needed.

4 Allow your stars to sit for a few days. The water will evaporate, leaving sparkly stars behind. You could tape the stars to a string to make a garland!

TIP Try making two star templates so your garland can have a variety of stars!

BOTTLE BLASTOFF

Vinegar and baking soda form a chemical reaction to send a rocket sky-high!

What You Need:

drinking straps

scissors

ruler

small plastic bottle

hot glue gun

construction paper

measuring cups
& spoons

vinegar

baking soda

paper towel

cork that will fit
in the bottle's
opening

funnel (optional)

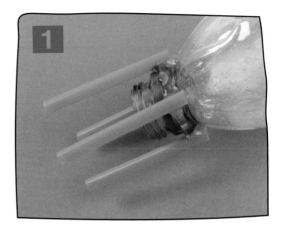

What You Do:

1 Cut four pieces of straw that are each 4 inches (10 cm) long. Glue them around the bottle's opening. Space them evenly.

2 Cut out construction paper flames. Glue them around the bottle's opening.

3 Put 1 cup (0.24 L) of vinegar in the bottle. Use a funnel if needed.

4 Put 2 tablespoons (30 mL) of baking soda on a paper towel. Fold the towel into a packet. Roll it up so it will fit in the bottle. Do not put it in the bottle yet!

5 Go to an area outside and away from people and buildings! Quickly stuff the packet into the bottle and push the cork into the opening. Turn the bottle upside down so it rests on the straws and step back. Watch your bottle blast off!

TIP Make your rocket more aerodynamic by gluing a funnel to the bottom of the bottle.

27

GUMMY GIRAFFE

Put your engineering skills to the test as you construct
a gummy creature that looks good enough to eat!

What You Need:

pretzel sticks

gummy candies

What You Do:

1. Push a pretzel stick into a gummy.

2. Push another pretzel stick into the gummy to connect the sticks.

3. Connect gummies and pretzels to make the giraffe's legs, neck, and head. Break pretzels into smaller pieces to make shorter segments.

4. Connect more gummies and pretzels to build a tree for your giraffe to munch on!

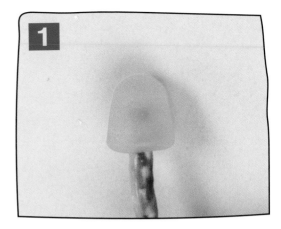

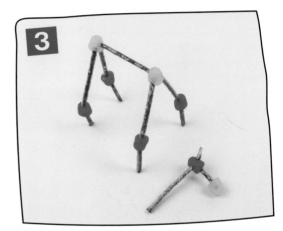

TIP Your gummy structures might be a bit wobbly. A larger base will help support your structures.

INVISIBLE INK

Use the power of citrus to craft a hidden design to give to a friend. Its contents will only be revealed when exposed to the heat of an iron!

What You Need:

lemon

sharp knife & cutting board

small bowl

cotton swab

paper

iron & ironing board

hair dryer (optional)

What You Do:

1 Cut the lemon in half and squeeze the juice into a small bowl.

2 Dip the cotton swab into the juice and use it to draw a design or write a message on the paper.

3 Let the juice dry completely, so you can no longer see your design.

4 Set an iron to high heat. Press it on the paper and slide it back and forth. This may take a few minutes. Soon, your design will be revealed!

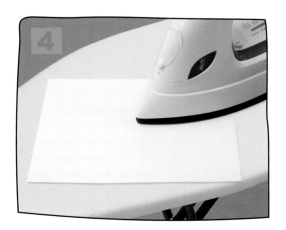

TIP Use a hair dryer to help the juice dry more quickly.

Read More

Bolte, Mari. *Super Science Projects You Can Make and Share*. North Mankato, MN: Capstone Press, 2016.

Rusick, Jessica. *Science Magic to Surprise and Captivate*. Minneapolis: Abdo Publishing, 2020.

Schuette, Sarah L. *10-Minute Science Projects*. North Mankato, MN: Capstone Press, 2020.

Internet Sites

Science Fun for Everyone!: Science Experiments for Kids
www.sciencefun.org/kidszone/experiments/

ThoughtCo.: Kitchen Science Experiments for Kids
thoughtco.com/kitchen-science-experiments-for-kids-604169

We Are Teachers: 55 Easy Science Experiments Using Materials You Already Have on Hand
weareteachers.com/easy-science-experiments/